Bullying

Rarely Travels Alone

Alan M. Davick, M.D.

Bullying: Rarely Travels Alone
Alan M. Davick, M.D.

© 2014 Alan M. Davick, M.D.

ISBN: 978-09890053-2-6

MISKIDDING, LLC
P.O. Box 101127
Cape Coral, FL 33910-1127

URL: www.DrDavick.com
Email: miskidding1@gmail.com

DISCLAIMER

This book is intended to be a guide to recognizing and managing bullying in children. It is not intended to be a recipe for diagnosing or treating physical or mental illness, nor does the purchase of this book establish in any way a professional relationship with the author or publisher.

The author and publisher are not responsible for the use or non-use of any diagnostic procedure, treatment option or choice of medication mentioned in this book. The reader is cautioned new information regarding diagnostic procedures, treatment options and medication-related information accumulates daily and may render the examples presented in this book outdated or even contraindicated by the date of publication. Therefore, the author and publisher do not assume and hereby disclaim any liability to any party for any loss, damage or disruption caused by error or omission in this book and associated websites or videos.

This book and associated websites and videos are not intended to replace medical, neurological, genetic, psychological or psychiatric advice tendered by the reader's own professional consultant(s) and the reader is strongly advised to discuss any pending decisions regarding diagnosis, treatment options or medication with such consultants.

Examples of bullying or victimization presented in this book are completely fictional and none of the characters, names or anecdotes are drawn from factual case histories. They are drawn from the author's experience over many years and any similarities between the characters, names or anecdotes used and actual case histories are purely coincidental.

Cover Photograph: Copyright Helder_Almeida|Dreamstime.com
Cover Design: www.RickFeeney.com

Acknowledgments

The principles presented in this book are distilled from the *MIS/KIDDING* Process®, published separately in *Managing Misbehavior in Kids: The MIS/KIDDING Process® - A Professionals' Manual.* They were developed by the author over many years of practice from colleagues in the fields of Medicine, Psychology and Education as well as from consultations with many families in distress. A complete listing of those who influenced this effort would easily double the size of this book!

The author shall limit mention of his gratitude to Rik Feeney, author, editor, publisher and coach, whose unfailing professionalism and ready advice has made the writing of this book a pleasure.

And, of course, to my wife, Barbara, whose patience seems limitless!

Al Davick

Preface

As a Behavioral-Developmental Pediatrician, perhaps ten percent of the families seeking my help identify bullying as at least one part of their problem. They may have a child who is a victim of bullying or they may "own" their own bully.

As the title suggests, bullying is almost never an isolated form of misbehavior. Indeed, other intense disorders typically accompany bullying and either fuel it or shield it from simple solutions. Some accompanying disturbances are "situational" and dissipate with counseling and time. Others are deeper seated and require more intense interventions. In this book, you learn when to suspect bullying, recognize its frequent behavioral traveling companions and how to manage its causes and effects.

Victims of bullying tend to exhibit intense anxiety or depression or refuse to engage in activities outside the home. Often, bullying first comes to parents' attention when a child refuses to attend school, if that's the scene of the bullying. Upon questioning or even spontaneously, a victimized child will identify the bully. Occasionally, a child will be fearful of reprisal and will hide the occurrence of bullying. In such cases, parents need to investigate and discover the cause of their children's sudden behavioral quirks.

Victims of bullying are chosen by perpetrators for a reason. The reason is always the same: Bullies recognize weaknesses in potential targets and bullies consciously or unconsciously anticipate their aggression will provide a soothing "balm" for their own psychological disturbances.

Many times, the vulnerabilities of victims are circumstantial. For example, a child who's just arrived in a new school or neighborhood may not yet have many or any friends who might act as a protective "herd" shielding the child from a potential bully.

Some of the vulnerabilities of victims can easily be eliminated, as with the making of friends or alignment with a group or clique. Other vulnerabilities, such as an unwillingness to confront a bully or to advise an authority of the problem, can be strengthened through counseling. But, sometimes victims suffer from underlying conditions over which they have little or no control. The most common vulnerabilities suffered by victims are depression, anxiety, poor self-esteem or self-loathing, deficient social skills and depressed mental age.

Bullies most commonly come to our attention because of complaints from others. Sometimes, victims will complain while at other times authorities, like teachers, other parents, neighbors or police officers, will lodge complaints.

Bullies, like victims, have reasons for their misbehavior. Such reasons include bullying's frequent traveling companions, like the poor choice-making of Oppositional-Defiant Disorder (ODD) – a mild form of defiance, or Conduct Disorder (CD) - a more intense and dangerous form of misbehavior. While poor choice-making always plays a major role in bullying, serious underlying mental health conditions, over which bullies have little or no direct control, can be insidious accompanying conditions of bullying. Bipolar Disorder, Intermittent Explosive Disorder and Borderline Personality Disorder are examples of underlying mental health disturbances commonly associated with bullying. Failure to recognize or manage these traveling companions of bullying will preclude a resolution of the problem.

Because bullying is so common, parents need to acquire simple, effective and timely strategies to recognize and manage bullying and any associated conditions, whether their children are victims or perpetrators. They need to:

- Identify bullying and any associated conditions

- Judge the severity of the misbehavior

- Recognize and eliminate or manage any underlying mental health conditions

- Develop strategies to control bullying

- Get their children to carry out the strategic goals

This book fills those needs. It's directed at nurturing parents who are not themselves bullies. I emphasize this because one frequent underlying cause of bullying in children is bullying by a parent. This book has no value to such a parent, though if one parent is the person from whom the child seeks protection and the other is a bully, the content of this book may, indeed, be useful.

Bullying: Rarely Travels Alone is a reference manual for parents and for children's caretakers, counselors and educators when their help is sought by parents for issues relating to bullying.

Introduction

Bullying is a form of aggressive behavior in which someone intentionally and repeatedly causes another person injury or discomfort. Bullying can take the form of physical contact, words or more subtle actions[1].

By definition, at least 2 individuals are involved in the misbehavior – the aggressor and the victim of the bullying. In some situations there may be a group of bullies acting together and there may be a group of victims.

Bullying can occur anywhere, including home, school, in the neighborhood or on the Internet. It's most frequently encountered in the elementary and middle school years. Boys more frequently exhibit this behavior than girls and, as perpetrators, present a higher risk of engaging in physical assaults. Boys are also more likely to be victims of physical assaults from bullying than girls. Girls are more likely to engage in cutting, usually an accompaniment of depression resulting from bullying, than boys. Girls also have a higher incidence of suicide as a result of bullying than boys.

Bullying is common and must be suspected and investigated whenever children exhibit unexplained anger, anxiety, depression, school refusal or sudden decline in school performance.

In Southwest Florida, a local newspaper, THE NEWS-PRESS, recently printed these statistics regarding bullying in 9th to 12th grade Florida students in 2011. The statistics are drawn from the Centers for Disease Control & Prevention's Youth Risk Behavior Survey[2]:

- 14% - Reported being bullied on school property

- 12% - Reported being electronically bullied

- 7 % - Didn't go to school at least once because they felt unsafe

- 26% - Felt sad or hopeless almost every day for 2 or more weeks

- 12% - Seriously considered suicide

You can see how bullying can be a complex and dangerous form of misbehavior. If you research it, you'll discover many professionals, including psychiatrists, psychologists, teachers, law enforcement and legal experts have been accumulating an astounding amount of information about bullying. Still, over the years, I've developed an approach to bullying and any associated conditions that cuts through professional jargon and theory. It simplifies the problem and offers a means of managing it.

In the chapters that follow, I'll show you how to:

- recognize a victim or a perpetrator of bullying

- judge the severity of bullying and any underlying conditions

- determine causes

- formulate a response

- get your child to stop bullying or being a victim

References:

1. American Psychological Association

2. Centers For Disease Control & Prevention's Youth Risk Behavior Survey

Table of Contents

Glossary of Terms

Bullying: Intentionally and repeatedly targeting another person with either physical or verbal aggression, resulting in injury or discomfort.[1]

Teasing: Intentionally and possibly repeatedly targeting another person with either physical or verbal aggression without causing injury or discomfort.

Traveling Companions of Bullying: Hidden physical or mental health disorders limiting appropriate choice-making by bullies or victims-

Adjustment Disorders- Potentially harmful emotional reactions to stressful events in a person's life, including poor self-esteem, self-loathing, depression, even suicide

Anxiety Disorders- The magnification of concern into worry, fear, even panic. In children the result may be withdrawal from required activities, isolation and school refusal. These disorders often fuel other mental health conditions.

Asperger Disorder- A form of autism affecting individuals with otherwise normal intelligence.

Autistic Spectrum Disorders- A group of disorders having in common deficiencies in social skills, communication skills and activities of daily living. The degree to which affected children achieve independence in later years depends upon their levels of intelligence and motivation.

Bipolar Disorders- A group of mental health conditions characterized by unstable emotions and variable degrees of stamina, often associated with a "disconnect" between one's acts and the consequences of those acts.

Borderline Personality Disorder- A mental health condition exhibiting emotional instability, irrational anger flare-ups and disordered interpersonal relationships, frequently associated with thoughts of suicide and often including superficial cutting and other forms of self-mutilation.

Conduct Disorder- A pattern of behavior consisting of persistent rule-breaking and defiant and aggressive acts disrupting physical health, social relationships, academic performance or authority relationships. Conduct disorders may themselves at times result from hidden mental health conditions that impair appropriate decision-making.

Depressive Disorder- A disturbance characterized by pervasive sadness or lack of interest in usual activities, sometimes associated with overeating or under-eating and resultant weight gains or weight loss, fatigue or sleeplessness, flagging self-esteem, poor focus and often thoughts of death or suicide. When these symptom persist for an extended period they qualify for a diagnosis of Major Depressive Disorder.

Intermittent Explosive Disorder- A disturbance of behavior in which an individual responds to minor or trivial events with exaggerated anger, fury or rage. Some episodes take the form of behavioral seizures.

Mood Disorder- A term applied to disturbances of emotion impacting on performance, relationships to other and authority, including spontaneous or exaggerated shifts in emotion and including either higher or lower than normal emotional states.

Oppositional-Defiant Disorder- Persistent inappropriate choices of behavior characterized by rule-breaking and defiance which, over extended periods, may progress to more serious Conduct Disorder.

Personality Disorders- A broad diagnostic group of character traits having in common the belief by affected individuals that their behaviors are normal or justified, but which disrupt activities of daily living, relationships to others, school or job performance and rule-following.

Situational Disorders- A general descriptive term applied to mental health disorders triggered by disruptive events in a person's life rather than by physical or genetically inherited conditions. Improvement and resolution of the disorder can be achieved by implementing effective management strategies with possible short-term use of medication.

Turner Syndrome- A genetic condition affecting girls and women in which all or part of an X sex chromosome is missing. Some of the features of the syndrome, such as shortness of stature, learning problems and overweight, often create vulnerabilities for bullying.

XYY Syndrome- A genetic condition affecting boys and med in which an extra Y sex chromosome in inherited. Some features of the syndrome, including tall stature and learning problems, may create vulnerabilities for bullying[2].

Consequence Areas Targeted by Bullying:

Objective (Observed) Measures of Bullying-

- Performance areas – the things "normal" children need to do to be normal.
    - o *physical* health - e.g. adequate stamina, growth
    - o *social* relationships – e.g. relating beneficially and effectively to others
    - o *educational* performance- e.g. achieving at one's level of ability
- Others reactions to children's behavior
- Authority relationships

Subjective (Emotional response by observers) Measures of Bullying-

- *annoyance*
- *Confusion*
- *Anger*
- *FEAR*

Bullying Thermometer- An easy way to visualize zones of intensity of bullying determined by point scores. High scores define life-threatening bullying which must be STOPPED immediately, low scores define teasing which may be ignored and mid-range scores allow time to construct management strategies.

Disciplinary Models for Implementing Management Strategies

Deterrence- "Stop [misbehaving] or [else]!" where [else] is a punishment.

Deflection- "If you obey we'll [reward] you; if you continue to disobey you will be [punished]."

Diversion- "If you obey, you may have [reward 1] or [reward 2]."

Drawing- "When you [obey] you get [reward 1] and when you continue to obey [reward 2, etc.]."

Sources of Power for Parents

Nurturance- All the things parents do to raise children.

Love- The things parents do for their children which are independent of their children's behavior or misbehavior and which allow children to grow and flourish. In its most basic form, food, shelter and clothing whether earned or unearned.

Affection- Things parents do for and with their children as a consequence of good behavior.

Sources of Motivation for Children

Rewards- Desirable consequences awarded for good behavior. They encourage more good behavior.

Bribes- Rewards given before they are earned or after misbehavior. They encourage misbehavior.

Professional Helpers

Physicians/Pediatricians- Medical doctors who diagnose and treat physical ailments in children. They are able to prescribe medications and hospitalize children.

Behavioral-Developmental Pediatricians- Physicians who have been trained as Pediatricians and who have additional training in recognizing and treating normal and abnormal brain development in children, especially physical and inherited conditions affecting child behavior.

Child Psychiatrists- Physicians with training in recognizing, diagnosing and treating disorders of the mind, including disturbances of neurological function, social relationships and personality disorders. Like other physicians, they can prescribe medications and hospitalize children.

Psychologists- Individuals trained to study, diagnose and treat the mind – both normal and abnormal conditions. They may have attained training at the Masters level, the Doctorate level or other degree level. They do not prescribe medications, though they may offer psychotherapy and may arrange a child's admission to a psychiatric hospital.

School Psychologists- Psychologists employed by schools or school systems. They offer measures of a child's intelligence, performance level, social skills and emotional state. These measures are used to construct an appropriate service plan for children with special needs.

Educators- A most diverse group of professionals focusing on the education of children. They include Principals, Teachers, School Counselors, Educational Specialists (e.g. math, speech and language, reading), Occupational and Physical Therapists, Audiologists and School Nurses. These professionals do not perform physical examinations, write prescriptions, give psychotherapy or hospitalize children. However, their ongoing observations of a child's physical, social and educational performance most often define bullying and any of its traveling companions.

Departments of Children and Families/Child Protective Services/Offices of Children and Families- State-sponsored agencies devoted to investigating and resolving issues related to child abuse and neglect. These agencies have authority to remove children from abusive or neglectful guardians and to initiate the provision of appropriate care to such children.

School Options

Boundary change- If your child has a medical, psychological or educational need that cannot be met at the current school, a Physician or Psychologist may request your child's transfer to a more appropriate school even if that school lies outside the boundaries of your geographical school district.

Charter or Magnet Schools- Public schools operating under contracts or "charters" allowing them more freedom to determine their curriculum, educational goals and the academic programs they use to achieve them. They are often very competitive and admission is often difficult.

Parochial/Private/Military Schools- Schools that establish their own admission criteria and are usually dependent on tuition charged to students, though fees may be adjusted to a family's finances. Discipline is often more stringent and military schools, in particular, may be lifesaving for some bullies.

Home/Hospital Program- Programs designed for children who are temporarily unable to attend school for physical or mental health disorders. Strict requirements are imposed for such programs, usually including a professional's evaluation, diagnosis and recommendation of duration of services.

Virtual (Cyber) School- full time accredited school programs which may be public or private and which span all grades. Internet technology allows students and teachers to interact from afar, within another part of the physical school or during a percentage of time at several sites. Children lacking social skills, as in autism and victims of bullying often benefits from this option until vulnerabilities have been managed or eliminated.

References
1. American Psychological Association

2. Gravholt, Claus Højbjerg (2013). "Sex chromosome abnormalities". In Pyeritz, Reed E.; Rimoin, David L.; Korf, Bruce R. *Emery and Rimoin's principles and practice of medical genetics* (6th ed.). San Diego

Chapter One

Recognizing Bullying and Its Traveling Companions

As with all forms of misbehavior, an initial question must be, "Is what I'm seeing misbehavior or is it normal behavior?" To answer that question, one might consult psychiatric journals, developmental tables, mathematical analyses of typical behaviors spanning the last several centuries... or, as I do, simply look at the consequences of the behavior. Over the years, I've limited my focus on the consequences of children's behaviors to the areas: effects on children's Performance, effects the behaviors have on Others and effects the behaviors have on children's relationships to Authority. Together, I call areas of Performance, Others and Authority the Consequence Areas:

- How does the behavior affect the child's Performance?

  Performance during the school years is itself judged in 3 areas: *physical* health, *social* relationships and *educational* performance. Normal performance in each of these subcategories can easily be compared to well-known standards for each age range[1].

- How does the behavior affect Others?

  This includes parents and family, but also teachers, neighbors, other kids, police – anyone. Effects on others are easily measured by the number of complaints generated by the others.

- How does the behavior affect Authorities?

  This, too, includes parents, teachers, other adults (babysitters, librarians, etc.), police - all authority figures. Behavioral effects on Authority can be recognized as appropriate or inappropriate rule-following.

Let's apply these tests of effects on the Consequence Areas to suspected bullying – either the suspicion of bullying or the suspicion of victimization. If you observe that the suspect behavior affects none of the Consequence Areas, what you're seeing is not bullying. Indeed, absent effects on any of the Consequence Areas, there's no misbehavior of any kind.

Here's an example:

Robert is 12 years old and lives with Mom, Dad and Trey, his younger, 8 year old brother. Trey is slightly overweight, Robert is not. Robert sometimes calls his younger brother, "fatso". Usually, this occurs when neither parent is present. Trey never responds to these taunts and on the rare occasion when his parents hear Robert comment, they tell Robert, "Please stop. That's not kind".

After several such episodes, Robert's Dad begins to wonder whether Robert is a bully. He's a bit anxious, reads this book and decides to begin by checking the Consequence Areas. He determines neither Robert nor Trey are failing to perform *physically* (good sleep, good appetite, good stamina), *socially* (affectionate to family [including Robert], attentive to friends, involved in all usual activities) and *educationally* (continuing to attend school without resistance and maintaining good grades). Both children are generating no complaints from Others, including each other, their friends, their teachers or anyone else. Nor is either child generating a complaint from any Authority, other than Dad.

If Dad chooses to complain as either an Other or as an Authority, he will have defined a low level of misbehavior – likely teasing, but possibly bullying. If he doesn't complain, there are truly no consequences to Robert's behavior and the behavior will merely qualify as teasing. This is a good example of a worthwhile adage for parents: Ignore things kids do that are merely mildly annoying when those behaviors have few or no ill consequences.

Now, let's move this example up a notch in intensity and see how it defines bullying for both victim and perpetrator.

We'll look in on the same family of Mom, Dad, 12 year old Robert and 8 year old Trey. This time, neither Mom nor Dad hears Robert say anything inappropriate to Trey. Instead, over the course of a few weeks, Trey begins to cry easily and has started to wet the bed at night. He requires Mom to physically accompany him to the bus stop each morning and sometimes must be cajoled into attending school. He repeatedly refuses to play with friends outside the house.

Trey's teacher calls to report he seems distracted and is failing to complete his work in class. Trey's behaviors, observed by the parents and reported by his teacher, are worrisome.

Separate and apart from concerns about Trey, the parents have received several written "referrals" from the school complaining Robert has been sent to the principal's office for cursing at his teachers after being disciplined for punching an autistic child in the lunchroom. Indeed, the school is considering suspending Robert or even transferring him to an Alternative Learning Center (a school for "behaviorally challenged" children).

A neighbor calls to report she saw Robert pushing and hitting Trey at the school bus drop-off point on 2 occasions. At home, Robert has been punished repeatedly for cursing, banging on walls, throwing and breaking dishes during episodes of rage, during which he seems out of control. Robert sleeps only a few hours at night, but teachers have reported he has been sleeping on his desk in school. He is never seen doing homework, but says he's passing all his subjects when asked. The parents have received a report card indicating Robert is failing all subjects but gym. Robert's Dad is angry at him and his Mom is fearful of the changes she sees in his behavior.

Limiting our examination of these events to the questions of whether Robert qualifies as a bully and whether Trey qualifies as a victim, we consult the Consequence Areas for each child:

Looking at Trey, the target of the bullying:

- All three components of Trey's Performance are affected: bedwetting is affecting his *physical* performance; crying over trivial events and insisting Mom accompany him to the school bus in front of his home are ill effects on Trey's *social* performance, which is also affected when he repeatedly refuses to play outside with friends; falling behind with school work is a deficiency of *educational* performance.

- Others are complaining of problems with Trey. They include his teacher and his parents.

- Authority would be affected if Trey refused to board his school bus and could not be cajoled into attending school.

23

With two and possibly all three of the Consequence Areas affected by Trey's behavior, there's no question his parents have encountered a serious problem. The parents may not yet know what we know about Robert targeting Trey, so identifying it as victimization from bullying may only be a suspicion at this point. Nonetheless, they know what they're seeing is not a trivial problem and it can't be ignored.

Looking at Robert, the bully:

- Robert's Performance is affected *physically* since he is unable to sleep and lacks stamina at school. His *social* relationships with parents and teachers are being threatened by his violent behaviors at home and at school. Robert's failing grades with the threat of his transfer to an Alternative Learning Program affect the *educational* area of his performance.

- Others, including teachers and parents are complaining of Robert's behaviors.

- Authority relationships are being challenged both at home and in school.

With all of the Consequence Areas affected by Robert's behavior, there's no doubt his parents are looking at a complex and serious problem. And there's no question that the bullying portion of the behavior goes well beyond the realm of teasing.

Now we've identified true examples of the "misbehavior" of bullying and see how measuring suspicious behaviors against the Consequence Areas defines any form of misbehavior, including bullying. Next we need to decide how much time we have to control these behaviors and their effects on victim and perpetrator. This is important because some victims are severely harmed either physically or emotionally, or even killed by assaults or suicide. Likewise, perpetrators may be severely harmed by underlying physical or mental health conditions or by the legal or extralegal consequences of their bullying. Indeed, potentially lethal outcomes may already be in play.

Let's Review What We've Learned in Chapter One

To identify misbehavior in school-aged children, including bullying, that may need to be managed:

Check the effects of suspicious behavior on the Consequence Areas:
- Performance areas
  - *physical* health
  - *social* relationships
  - *educational* performance

- Complaints from Others
  - You
  - Anyone else

- Threats to Authority

If any of these Consequence Areas are affected, the behavior must be considered worthy of attention and cannot (yet) be ignored.

References:
1. Davick AM, Managing Misbehavior in Kids: The *MIS*/Kidding Process[®], 2014

Chapter Two

Judging the Severity of Bullying and Associated Misbehavior

In this chapter, we identify bullying and associated conditions that may be life threatening to either victim or bully and which must be STOPPED immediately. We learn which forms of bullying are of so little consequence that they may be considered merely teasing – worthy of monitoring lest they intensify to a higher level, but deserving of no immediate action.

Here we'll learn how to STOP life endangering misbehavior and ignore trivial forms of teasing. When we're done, we'll be able to focus our efforts solely on disturbances that might potentially escalate to life endangering levels if ignored, but which leave us time to develop strategies for their management.

As the effects of bullying impact more of the Consequence Areas, the more dangerous it becomes. This applies equally to victims and perpetrators. When all three of the Consequence areas – Performance, Others, Authority - are affected, bullying may reach a life-threatening level.

Counting the number of Consequence Areas affected by misbehavior such as bullying is an objective measure of intensity. There's another way to judge severity. We can judge the intensity of our feelings as we observe misbehavior. Our feelings may range from annoyance through Confusion, Anxiety or Anger, to outright FEAR. Emotions vary as we watch misbehavior because we are unconsciously calculating potential outcomes. This process, based on the intensity of our emotional responses to misbehavior, is a subjective measure of severity.

Consciously applying these objective and subjective measures of severity to bullying and any associated misbehavior is an effective way to predict deadly outcomes before they occur. Anticipating life-endangering bullying can prevent injury or death to victim, perpetrator or others. The bullying thermometer is especially useful when a high risk of death is not intuitively apparent. For example, Trey, not yet identified as a victim of bullying, but experiencing disturbance of all three Consequence Areas in the intense example above might attempt suicide, though no one has heard him threaten to do so. Robert, also experiencing involvement of all three Consequence Areas, might commit homicide or suicide.

Let's look at this process of judging severity a bit more closely.

Objective Measures of Severity

Here's a diagram showing the various components of the Consequence Areas. Counting all the parts of the Consequence Areas affected by a misbehavior is an objective measure of its severity. In this diagram, I've assigned degrees to each component of the Consequence areas:

The Consequence Areas

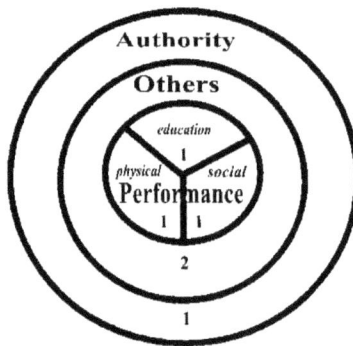

When bullying affects Performance, each subcategory of performance is given 1 degree. When Others are complaining, both you and anyone else affected are each given 1 degree for a possible total of 2 degrees. When anyone's Authority is affected, 1 degree is assigned.

Thus a maximum of 6 degrees might be generated by the effects of bullying on the Consequence Areas.

Now we'll look at feelings as a subjective measure of the intensity of bullying.

Subjective Measures of Severity

Here's a table of emotions most people experience when they observe teasing or bullying. Degrees have been designated for the intensity of each level of emotional response:

Emotional Response	Level of Intensity	Degrees
annoyance	mild reaction	1
Confusion, Anxiety, Anger	Moderate reaction	2
FEAR	SEVERE reaction	3

Not everyone will experience the same emotional reaction to a bullying situation, but my experience has shown most parents and other observers are remarkably consistent in judging trivial misbehaviors by the mere *annoyance* they generate. Likewise, most observers are consistent with the judgment of severe misbehaviors by the *FEAR* they generate. It's within the middle group of *Confusion, Anxiety or Anger* that differences in emotional response most often occur. In my opinion, the emotions of the middle group as a whole share roughly the same level of intensity. Accordingly, I assign 1 degree to annoyance, 2 degrees to Confusion, Anxiety or Anger and 3 degrees to FEAR. Only the most intense reaction experienced by an observer of bullying and its effects is chosen to score this subjective test. For example, watching bullying in action might generate Anxiety, Anger and FEAR, but fear would be selected to score the subjective measure.

Now we'll combine objective and subjective degrees as a scoring system to define the intensity of bullying. This will allow us to ignore mere teasing, unworthy of immediate intervention because of its lack of significant consequences. We'll quickly be able to recognize life-endangering bullying before it seriously harms or kills someone. We need to do this because once recognized, such bullying must be STOPPED immediately with whatever means are available.

Combining the observed number of observed consequences (an objective measure) with an estimate of the intensity of the observer's emotions (a subjective measure) is an accurate way to determine if action must be taken and how soon it need be taken. High combined scores mean bullying must be STOPPED immediately. Extremely low scores can be ignored or monitored without other action. Intermediate scores mean bullying is potentially dangerous, but there is time to figure out how to manage it.

I've found the following temperature ranges useful to distinguish teasing from moderately disruptive bullying and to identify life-endangering threat levels:

A Bullying Thermometer

- Life-threatening bullying $7 - 9°$

- Moderate levels of bullying

  (with time for strategies) $3 - 6°$

- Teasing $1 - 2°$

Using the examples we saw in Chapter One, we'll apply this scoring system and see how it works.

Applying an Objective Score to the Bullying of Trey

Let's begin by revisiting Trey in the first scenario presented in Chapter One. You may recall his older brother calls him, "Fatso", from time to time. We'll test the effects of Robert's taunts on Trey's behavior. We'll check Trey's reactions against the Consequence Areas, beginning with his Performance.

- No problems with Trey's *physical* performance = 0°

- Trey's *social* performance is unaffected   =0°

- No known consequences to Trey's *educational* performance

        =0°

Now we check Trey's behavior against Others.

- No Others are complaining about Trey   =0°

Last, we check Trey's behavior against Authority.

- No Authority figure is being challenged =0°

Total Objective Score =0°

Applying Feelings as Subjective Scores for Bullying of Trey

In this example, the only individual concerned with the consequences of Robert's comments to Trey is Dad. He may be *annoyed* (1 degree) with Robert, but certainly not with Trey; thus the 1 degree would apply to Robert, not Trey. Or, he may be *Anxious* about Trey's reaction to Robert's comments (2 degrees). Since Dad's anxiety relates to Trey, the degrees are applied to Trey. We'll get to Robert shortly, but Trey's total score is no greater than 2 degrees (objective = 0 + subjective = 2). Consulting the Bullying Thermometer shown above, we see this temperature defines trivial teasing and can, for the time being, be ignored. If the teasing continues or intensifies, it may begin to create consequences for Trey that will yield a higher score, propelling Dad to action.

Next, we'll apply these measures to Robert in the first scenario.

Applying the Counting of Consequences to Robert as an Objective Score

Robert is teasing Trey by calling him, "Fatso". His parents have told him to stop teasing – it isn't kind. Nonetheless, Robert persists. Though we see Trey suffering no measurable consequences (yet), Robert's actions will now be examined. As before, we test Robert's behavior against the Consequence Areas, beginning with Robert's Performance:

- No problem with Robert's *physical* performance   =0°
- Robert's *social* performance is unaffected   =0°
- No known effect on Robert's *educational* performance

=0°

Now we check Robert's behavior against Others.

- Parents have complained at Robert   =2°

Last, we check Robert's behavior against Authority.

- Robert has disregarded his parents' directive to stop teasing

=1°

Total Objective Score =3°

Applying Emotional Reactions as a Subjective Score to Robert

In the first scenario, Dad has become a bit anxious about Robert's failure to stop teasing Trey. His *Anxiety* generates 2 degrees on the subjective scale. Adding the objective score of 3 degrees and the subjective score of 2 degrees, Dad is looking at a total score of 5 degrees – consistent with a moderate level of bullying. Dad has learned that moderate levels of misbehavior (such as bullying, in this instance) will, over time, lead to ever greater consequences for Robert. Yes, that's NOT A TYPO! Robert, as the perpetrator, will suffer the consequences of his bullying, whether or not his victim does. Those consequences could include restrictions, loss of privileges, punishments, even psychotherapy (which from Robert's perspective, would likely be considered a punishment.)

The longer the bullying persists, the more complaints it generates from Others and Authority (higher objective scores) and the higher the degree of an observer's emotional response (higher subjective scores.) These higher bullying scores require ever more intense interventions.

Robert's misbehavior score of 5 degrees qualifies as a moderate level of bullying. Dad knows moderate levels of bullying require a strategy for control and he knows he'll have some time to develop the strategy. If the score had reached life-endangering levels of 7–9 degrees, the bullying would have to be STOPPED immediately, with forceful intervention.

If, instead of feeling *Anxiety* (2 degrees), Dad had merely felt *annoyance* (1 degree) at Robert's behavior and no one, as an Other, had complained, Robert's combined bullying score would have fallen 3 degrees to an overall score of 2 degrees. A glance at the Bullying Thermometer would show this score qualifies as mere teasing. Teasing can be ignored until or unless it escalates to a higher level.

Now we'll examine the more troublesome events in the second account presented in Chapter One. This narrative, in which Robert is again the bully and Trey the victim, provides an opportunity for us to learn when and how to STOP life-threatening bullying and its potentially life-endangering consequences for the victim.

As before, we'll begin with Trey.

Counting Consequences to a Victim as an Objective Score of Bullying

We begin with a look at the effects of bullying on Trey's Consequence Areas starting with Performance.

- Trey cries too easily, wets the bed, seems distracted – all effects on Trey's *physical* performance $=1°$

- Trey's new demand for Mom to walk him to the bus and his refusal to play with friends are effects on *social* performance

$=1°$

- Trey' *educational* performance is reported to be falling behind $=1°$

A look at complaints from Others includes Trey's teacher.

- Trey's teacher complains he seems distracted $=1°$

If Trey refuses to go to school, (parents') Authority is affected

$(+/-1°)$

Total Objective Score $=4-5°$

Adding Observers Feelings as a Subjective Measure of Trey's Victimization

Observing Trey's behavior and receiving a concerning report from Trey's teacher, the parents have become *Anxious*. $=2°$

If Trey was not refusing to attend school, thus avoiding a degree from threat to Authority, his total combined (Objective + Subjective) bullying score would be 6°. This score, falling at the highest end of the moderate range would leave his parents time to develop a strategy to manage the problem.

If Trey were to refuse to go to school, the effect on Authority would add an additional degree to his bullying score, which would increase to 7 degrees. His score would then enter a life-endangering range (7 – 9 degrees) of victimization. His parents would need to STOP his victimization immediately, before considering any strategy to decrease his vulnerability.

Now we'll use the Bullying Thermometer to measure the intensity of Robert's misbehavior in the second account. As you read that scenario, you may not have realized how dangerous Robert's bullying has become. You may also not have realized his or his victim's life could be in danger. The true value of determining a bullying score will become apparent with the next example.

Counting Consequences as an Objective Score of Robert's Bullying

Consequence Areas affected by Robert's bullying as described in the second sketch in Chapter One:

- Performance is affected in all 3 of its subcategories:
  o Rages out of control, wakefulness at night and sleeping in school are all examples of disturbance in the *physical* component. $=1°$
  o Cursing, disrespect of adults affect *social* component. $=1°$
  o Failing grades, behavioral referrals affect *education*. $=1°$

- Others are complaining and are directly affected by Robert's misbehavior, including teachers, parents, and other children. $=2°$
- Authority of teachers, parents being challenged. $=1°$

Total Objective Score $=6°$

Adding the *Subjective* Measure of Robert's Bullying

Robert's Dad is *Angry* at Robert's oppositional and disrespectful behavior. Mom is *FEAR*ful of the changes she sees in her son. Scoring these emotions, we select the most intense reaction, *FEAR,* and thus derive 3 degrees.

Total Combined Score $=9°$

Robert's parents, having read this book, now know they are facing a life-endangering level of bullying. This means they must STOP the bullying immediately with whatever means are required.

How We STOP Life-Threatening Bullying

A bullying score of 9 degrees defines a life-endangering level of misbehavior. It must be STOPPED immediately with whatever means are required. The parents of the bully have the authority and the wherewithal to intervene forcefully in these situations. Though they themselves may not have license to impose physical restraints on a combative child nor may they have the skills mental health professionals possess, they can authorize intervention by such individuals. Appropriate forms of voluntary and involuntary intervention are discussed below.

Deciding How Much Time You Have to STOP Victimization

Parents whose child is a victim, but who have no direct authority over the bully, can appeal to those who have direct authority to intervene immediately. However, depending upon the extent of the commitment of those authorities to stop the bullying and depending upon the "temperature" experienced by their victimized child, parents may need to REMOVE THEIR CHILD FROM DANGER, rather than wait for a response from those with authority over the bully. Bullying scores of 7 – 9 degrees fall in this category.

Moderate bullying scores of 3 – 6 degrees allow time to work with authorities like teachers, the bully's parent(s) and possibly directly with the bully. The effects of moderate bullying leave time to investigate a victim's vulnerabilities, as discussed in the next chapter, and to manage or eliminate them. Moderate levels of bullying leave time to fully define and possibly overcome the victim's vulnerabilities. How this is done is also presented in the next chapter.

Before we learn how to discover and manage underlying conditions over which bullies and their victims have little or no direct control, let's be sure to STOP life-threatening bullying immediately.

How to STOP Life-Endangering Victimization

When a victimized child generates a score of 7 – 9 degrees on the Bullying Thermometer, a life-endangering situation exists which may result in physical harm or life-endangering psychological damage to that child. Depending upon the circumstances, one or another of the following steps may be taken:

- When a bully is causing physical harm or has just caused physical harm, a **911** call is justified.

Most commonly, this will result in a police visit to the scene. A report will be generated detailing the facts. If the bully is found to be uncooperative or violent, forceful detention may follow. Police officers, physicians and psychologists may determine the bully is seriously enough disturbed that voluntary or involuntary admission to a child psychiatric facility is warranted to stabilize and possibly treat underlying vulnerabilities.

- When emotional trauma is resulting in a bullying score of 7-9 degrees, in the life-threatening range, *the victim must be removed from the vicinity of the bully* until vulnerabilities have been identified and eliminated or managed (as in the next chapter).

Here are some ways to remove a victim from a bully's vicinity until vulnerabilities have been identified and managed. Do not depend upon your child to achieve these steps. These are adult decisions and acts.

- For exposure at school notify the teacher and the principal of the problem and keep records of the dates, encounters and participants in any meetings you have with authorities. These documents may become important if legal steps are contemplated in the future. Determine if you're satisfied with the responses of those to whom you appeal. If not, document your reactions in writing.

- Discuss the problem with the parent(s) of the bully, if possible and document such discussions with the parent(s), since these may become important if legal steps are contemplated in the future. See if safety can be immediately established for your child.

- You may need to remove your child from the class or school while you arrange the longer-term removal of your child from the bully or bullies.

- You may need to request a change of classroom/teacher, depending on the age of your child.

- You may need to consider transferring your child from the school, especially if there are several bullies involved or the school fails to act responsibly. You might:

  - apply for a boundary change – this a formal agreement by the school to allow your child to attend another school outside your geographic district. It requires medical or psychiatric documentation of the destructive and dangerous effects of the bullying on your child.

  - consider a charter school or a private school outside the public system, such as a parochial school.

  - consider Virtual School (computer program coordinated with the school's curriculum, but outside the physical confines of the school.)

  - consider a temporary Home/Hospital program (requiring a psychologist's or physician's examination and authorization.)

For exposure in the neighborhood:

- Speak with the parent(s) of the bully about the problem, if possible. Document any discussions since these may become important if legal steps are contemplated in the future. See if safety can be established for your child.

- It may also be necessary to restrict your child's activities outside the home when adult supervision is unavailable.

- Consider a voluntary psychiatric admission for your child if anxiety, depression, cutting, drug abuse or suicidal thinking is encountered. Though such a decision may not be met with enthusiasm by your child, it could be truly life-saving. Remember, these are adult decisions, so don't wait for your child's approval.

How to STOP Life-Endangering Bullying

Bullies don't come with labels and they rarely complain to their parents of a compulsion to bully. However, bullies do behave in ways which register on the Bullying Thermometer. Suspicion of bullying is most often generated by complaints about the child from others, sometimes including the victim. When scores above 2 on the scale are encountered by a parent, whether bullying is unsuspected or is under consideration, intervention is required.

Scores between 3 and 6 indicate FOR THE BULLY ONLY that there is time to uncover causes and to develop a strategy for management. THIS DOES NOT ELIMINATE THE POSSIBILITY THAT THE VICTIM MAY BE AT CRITICAL RISK. Once bullying has been identified at any level, a parent has the duty to approach the victim or the victim's custodian to determine the degree of trauma experienced by the victim and to assist in whatever way possible with the prevention of further trauma.

Bullying scores of 7 – 9, indicating a life-endangering threat level to the bully, require immediate action to STOP the bullying and prevent potentially lethal consequences FOR THE BULLY as well as for the victim.

The safety of all concerned requires the physical removal of the bully from the vicinity of the victim.

Here are some ways to STOP life-threatening bullying by your child:

- **Call to authority**- If your child is in the act of physically injuring a victim, immediate removal of your child from the vicinity of the victim is critical. If your child is rebellious or too big for you to handle, a **911** call is appropriate. Most commonly, this will result in a police visit to the scene. A report will be generated detailing the facts. If your child is uncooperative or violent, forceful detention may follow. Police officers, physicians and psychologists may determine your child is seriously enough disturbed that admission to a child psychiatric facility is warranted to stabilize and possibly treat underlying conditions.

- **Removal from the arena**- If your child has been physically harming victim(s), both the child and the victim(s) remain in danger, especially if an underlying mental health condition is causative, unrecognized or untreated. Under such circumstances, it's reasonable for you to arrange the admission of your child to a child psychiatric facility for a brief cool-down and professional assessment. This is far better than risking a 911 call and having a police record established for your child. It's also far better than risking retaliation against your child by a misguided adult.

- **Get professional help**- Children who bully in and out of school or on the internet are usually carrying underlying mental health conditions wherever they go. This type of bullying cannot be managed by discipline alone. Punishment often intensifies the bullying by fueling anger which is then directed at victims. Children who engage in bullying as a pattern of behavior require evaluation and treatment by a psychologist or psychiatrist and many will require medication management.

  Schools often respond to bullying by transferring a bully to an Alternative Learning Center (ALC) where children with behavior problems are closely supervised. Such schools typically focus more on behavioral management than on academic performance. If, as a result of bullying, your child is transferred to an ALC, falling behind academically and exposure to unsavory role models may follow. A proactive approach, such as consultation with a psychologist or psychiatrist or even a brief admission to a child psychiatric facility, is preferable to depending upon a school to solve a bullying problem.

Here are some ways to STOP life-endangering victimization from bullying:
- **Calls to authority-**
  - When immediate physical danger is not present, speaking with your child's teacher and the school principal may result in the immediate supervision and monitoring of the bully as well as your child.

  - Advising your child's pediatrician of the bullying problem and getting a note from the physician requesting forceful and timely intervention from the school can be helpful.

o   When assaults are a part of the bullying and especially when injury has been sustained by your child, a call to Department of Children and Families (DCF) reporting abuse is advisable. If a child reports the immediate aftermath of an assault, a **911** call is justified.

- **Removal from the arena-**

  o   When physical assaults are targeting your child, immediate removal from the classroom is advisable. Keeping your child at home until the bullying has been effectively controlled through consultation with the school authorities is a reasonable first step. Missing a few days from school while work is provided at home may allow the bullying situation to be managed. However, missing school for any length of time will intensify your child's victimization by imposing hardship on the victim rather than the bully.

  o   When a teacher, principal or school fails to act decisively to protect your child, a change of class, a change of school or enrollment in an alternative educational program may be required. Here are some options:

    - **Boundary Exception-** When a bullying environment cannot be adequately purged, either because of a non-committal school staff or because of a dominant school culture, moving your child to another school outside your geographic district may be the best course of action. Within the public school system, moving out of the district is known as a Boundary Exception. It requires written documentation of ongoing medical, psychological or psychiatric trauma to your child.

    - **Virtual School-** This is a program in which the mainstream curriculum is presented by computer. The enrollment may be full-time or part-time and should be considered appropriate only so long as a bullying situation remains unresolved. Lengthy enrollment in Virtual School can lead to computer addiction and lagging social skills.

- **Home/Hospital Program**- When a victim of bullying has suffered either physical or mental injury requiring ongoing, intense therapy, providing a home-based curriculum can life-saving. Over time, this option, like Virtual School, can lead to isolation and intensify a child's anxiety about returning to a mainstream school.

- Get professional help for underlying vulnerabilities

  o Situational conditions like the isolation of a newcomer to a classroom, school, or neighborhood can be managed by encouraging healthy friendships, involvement in team activities and neighborhood activities.

  o Learning disabilities and comprehension problems require special educational services.

  o Mental health conditions like anxiety, depression and autistic disorders require assessment and treatment by psychologists or psychiatrists.

Before you move on to Chapter Three, where you discover how to uncover and manage the vulnerabilities and mental health conditions often associated with bullying, let's take stock of what you've already learned.

In Chapter One, you examined the Consequence Areas, which you can use to separate trivial teasing from bullying. In Chapter Two, you've seen how to judge the severity of bullying and STOP life-endangering levels. Having STOPPED the immediate threat of further harm to victim or perpetrator, you've placed life-endangered children under the scrutiny of professionals.

Now you're left with moderate levels of bullying or victimization. These levels of bullying or victimization cannot be ignored and may eventually lead to life-endangering levels if unresolved in a timely fashion. However, moderate levels of bullying do allow time to develop strategies for their control. But, before you begin to construct strategies, you'll need to make one additional determination. Is your child physically and emotionally able to stop bullying or to eliminate vulnerabilities or are underlying physical or mental conditions present over which your child has no control?

Chapter Three shows you a simple and effective way to make this determination.

Let's Review What We've Learned in Chapter Two

To judge the severity of bullying and any associated misbehavior:

- Determine the objective score of the bullying by checking the misbehavior against the Consequence Areas and assigning degrees- *see diagram page 28.*

    o Performance areas: Up to 3°

    - *Physical* $=1°$
    - *Education* $=1°$
    - *Social* $=1°$

    o Effects on Others: Up to 2°

    - *You* $=1°$
    - *Anyone else* $=1°$

    o Effect on Authority: Up to 1°

- Determine the subjective score of the bullying by estimating your emotional reaction. Choose only the most intense reaction to score- *see table on page 29.*

- Combine objective and subjective scores to determine total degrees: *see thermometer on page 30.*

    o 7 – 9° defines SEVERE bullying which may be life-threatening and which must be STOPPED immediately. Options include:

    - Calls to authority

    - Removal of the bully or victim from the arena

    - Getting professional help

    o 3 – 6° defines Moderate bullying which cannot be ignored, but leaves time for developing a management strategy

    o 1 – 2° defines teasing and may be ignored

Chapter Three

Identifying Causes, Vulnerabilities & "Conditions"

Now we've learned to identify bullying and victimization and to add point estimates of their objective and subjective consequences. Using the Bullying Thermometer we've sorted bullying with any associated misbehavior into mild, moderate or severe levels. Choosing among the options presented in the last chapter, we've STOPPED life-endangering bullying and we've recognized and are safely ignoring mere teasing. We're now left with moderate forms of bullying which give us time to discover causes and develop strategies for their control.

Our focus in this chapter is to further limit bullying and victimization to bad decision-making by eliminating underlying mental health conditions over which the bully or victim have no control. This is a critical step because we can't assign total responsibility to children for decision-making if underlying conditions have taken away their ability to make choices. We'll soon see how we can redirect bad choice-making, but this is possible only after we manage or eliminate underlying disorders and are sure bullies or victims are free to make better choices.

Mental disorders may fuel bad behavior and, from a bully's viewpoint, force the choice of bullying as a misguided attempt to lessen the impact of the disorder. Typical conditions underlying bullying include bullying at home, poor self-esteem and mood disorders.

As for victims, underlying depression, anxiety, poor self-esteem or self-loathing, deficient social-adaptive skills and other intellectual deficits, are often targeted by bullies. These disturbances often lead victims to accept and even encourage victimization. When victims shed such susceptibilities, their victimization usually ends.

Some mental conditions, like mood disorders, can be accurately diagnosed and effectively treated. Some, like Autistic Spectrum Disorders, may have long-lasting consequences for a child and may require intense, long-term counseling or therapy. Children suffering from chronic conditions may require lifelong protection from bullying.

When mental disorders have been identified and treated or eliminated, free choice-making is restored and parents and other authorities can redirect their children's behavioral choices.

Though as a parent you may not be able to diagnose specific mental health conditions, you can easily discern their presence. Once a mental disorder is suspected, an appropriate professional can be employed to diagnose and treat it. Here follow some tools I've found useful to recognize the presence of mental health disorders that limit children's choice-making.

How to Recognize Underlying Mental Disorders in Bullies

Mental disorders that underlie bullying don't switch on and off from one place to another. They are non-selective; that is, they occur everywhere and under any circumstances. In the case of mood disorders, for example, these disturbances are seen not only where the bullying occurs, but everywhere. When a bully attempts to lessen the impact of an underlying mental health disorder by choosing to bully, both the underlying condition and the bullying follow the child everywhere.

Let's review an example of this principle at work in the second sketch we encountered in Chapter One.

Recall that Robert, 12 years of age, has generated complaints from school, from a neighbor and at home. He's been cursing at teachers, sleeping during class, failing academically and punched an autistic child at school. A neighbor complained to Robert's parents that she saw Robert pushing and hitting his younger brother, Trey, at the bus stop. At home, Robert has been having sleepless nights and engages in violent rages during which he curses, breaks dishes and punches walls.

These behaviors are occurring everywhere and are having harmful consequences for Robert, aside from any impact they may have on others.

Although we suspect Robert is bullying Trey, we can easily observe that Robert's behavior is repetitious wherever he goes. Before we consider disciplining Robert, we need to identify and manage underlying disturbances over which he may have little or no control. We'll see how that's done after we apply the same yardstick to Trey, the victim.

How to Recognize Underlying Mental Disorders in Victims

In the sketch we revisited, Trey is observed to cry easily, has begun wetting the bed, is refusing to go to school, is afraid to leave the house alone and avoids playing with friends. His teacher has reported his schoolwork is lagging and he seems distracted in class.

Though these observations might suggest a bullying problem, Trey is exhibiting behaviors occurring in all venues with harmful consequences to him. Before trying to equip Trey to develop defensive strategies for bullying, we need to identify and manage any underlying disturbances over which Trey has little or no control. Otherwise, our efforts to end Trey's victimization are doomed to failure.

Just as in the example of Trey's behavior, the consequences of Robert's behavior are harmful to him and to others and are occurring in many circumstances and locations. He's exhibiting anger at home and at school and his rages seem out of proportion to any triggering events.

So What Do ALL Underlying Conditions Have in Common?

Underlying disorders exhibit their effects in all locations, at unpredictable times and result in harmful consequences for the child as well as for others. This is different from willful misbehavior which selects targets, occurs only in relation to the targets and (from the perpetrator's view) achieves a desired, though misguided, consequence. Here's a summary of the differences between underlying mental health conditions and willful misbehavior:

Underlying Conditions	Willful Misbehavior
• Occur everywhere	• Selective location
• No single target	• Targets someone/thing
• No apparent benefit to child	• Misguided goal is apparent

What to Do When Underlying Mental Disorders Are Suspected

The conditions that often underlie bullying and victimization are not limited in their expression to bullying. Underlying causes and vulnerabilities are best viewed through the broader lens of misbehavior affecting the Consequence Areas. As you've learned in Chapter One, misbehavior affecting the Consequence Areas of Performance, Others or Authority at a moderate or life-endangering level requires intervention. High intensity misbehavior must be STOPPED immediately.

Moderate level bullying leaves time for the exploration of underlying causes or vulnerabilities, as you've just learned. Once these hidden disorders have been recognized and managed, you'll be able to devise strategies to induce your child to control bullying and its effects.

When you suspect hidden mental disorders, you'll need professional help to sort them out and either accommodate to them or eliminate them.

Which Professionals to Use For Suspected Underlying Conditions

I like to divide professional consultants for bullying into three groups – Physicians, Psychologists and Educators. Each group has different capabilities. To help us choose among these consultants, we need only identify affected components of the Consequence Areas. Here's how it's done:

- A Physician should first be consulted when you suspect an underlying cause of bullying. That's because misbehavior affecting the Performance component of the Consequence Areas (*physical, social, educational*) may relate to physical illness and medical doctors can identify and treat such conditions. Examples of the many physical conditions that may underlie bullying include lead or mercury poisoning, thyroid under or over activity and genetic disorders, like Turner Syndrome or XYY Syndrome.

- Psychologists can next measure social maturity (a core area of difficulty in Autistic Spectrum Disorders), intelligence (including specific learning disabilities), emotional disorders, attention deficits and achievement levels. This type of testing, called psychometrics, costs in the range of $500 when done privately, but are free services when provided by a child's school. Psychologists can help develop strategies for coping with underlying disorders (like mood disorders, autistic disorders, etc.) and they can provide therapy and counseling.

- Educators, including teachers, principals, reading and math specialists, speech and language specialists, occupational therapists and school counselors, can manage school safety, provide an appropriate curriculum for the specific educational needs uncovered by Physicians and Psychologists and can track a child's progress with achievement tests and behavioral observations. They often act as critical eyes through which other professionals follow children's responses to interventions.

In general, when underlying disorders are suspected, professionals are best utilized in this order:

Physicians > Psychologists > Educators.

Let's examine some examples of how professionals might be of critical importance for Trey and Robert in the previously presented sketches. Though the examples that follow name some common underlying conditions, the possibilities in any case of bullying are almost limitless. They all have one thing in common. Medical and mental health conditions steal the ability to make appropriate behavioral choices from children and render discipline and strategies ineffective.

Trey Is Experiencing *physical* Consequences from Bullying > Physician

Trey's parents observe he has begun wetting the bed. His teacher notes he seems unfocused in class. Before assuming Trey's behavior is under his control, his parents arrange for Trey to be examined by his Pediatrician.

In this case, Trey's examination by his Pediatrician is normal. I've seen cases where bedwetting and wetting in school were due to urinary tract disease and where victimization from bullying resulted from incontinence in school. It's never a good idea to assume that problems in the area of *physical* performance are psychological in origin.

Trey Is Experiencing *social* Consequences from Bullying > Psychologist

Trey's parents suspect he suffers from depression. They arrange next for the School Psychologist to meet with Trey. The Psychologist does, indeed, diagnose depression. Trey confides that he is being bullied by his older brother, Robert, but also by several of Robert's classmates. He's able and willing to identify the boys by name.

The Psychologist advises the principal of the specifics. The principal and Psychologist meet with the bullies, advise their parents of the situation and warn the boys that additional complaints will result in their suspension from school.

Trey meets weekly with the Psychologist for several weeks. A determination is made that Trey's depression is situational; that is, caused by stressful events rather than due to inherited or brain chemical imbalances. During his sessions with the Psychologist, Trey makes progress at home and at school. The bedwetting stops, outside activities resume and schoolwork improves.

Trey Is Experiencing *educational* Consequences from Bullying > Educator

Trey's school refusal and lagging school performance initially prompt his parents to meet with his teacher. The teacher had no direct knowledge of bullying. However, the teacher's observations provided the parents with several of the objective disturbances in the

Consequence Areas. These effects, along with the parents' emotional response to Trey's behavior, defined a moderate level of bullying and triggered the parents' interventions.

Trey responds to the school's identification and management of the bullying as well as his sessions with the Psychologist. The principal and the teacher, both Educators, track Trey's progress. They act as eyes and ears for the parents and the Psychologist. Should bullying resume, these Educators would be among the first to observe and report its consequences.

Now let's take a look at how Robert's parents assess possible underlying conditions in Robert's bullying before they move on to constructing a strategy. They know some causes of bullying are not under a child's direct control and must be eliminated before they can hold Robert fully responsible for bad decision-making.

Robert Is Exhibiting *physical* Consequences to Performance > Physician

Robert's sleeping in class and sleeplessness at home are examples of *physical* disturbance to the Performance subcategory of the Consequence Areas. His parents schedule an examination with his Pediatrician. The Pediatrician finds no specific abnormality.

Robert Is Exhibiting *social* Consequences to Performance > Psychologist

Recall that Robert has been experiencing sleepless nights and has been engaging in violent rages during which he curses, breaks dishes and punches walls. He fights with other students and has attacked Trey, generating complaints from a neighbor. These are examples of disturbance within the *social* area of Performance. The parents next arrange for the School Psychologist to assess Robert's behavior.

The Psychologist meets with Robert on three occasions and conveys to the parents his suspicion that Robert suffers from Bipolar Disorder. He advises consultation with a Child Psychiatrist.

Robert's parents follow through with the Psychologist's recommendation. After several sessions with the Child Psychiatrist, a definitive diagnosis is made and the Psychiatrist advises psychotherapy and medication to stabilize Robert's mood disturbance and sleep disorder.

Robert Exhibits Disturbance in the *education* Area of Performance > Educator

The school schedules a meeting with Robert's parents. The Principal, School Psychologist and Robert's teacher are in attendance.

Robert's verbal assaults on his teacher in school and his physical assault on an autistic child in school resulted in his suspension. At that time, Robert's parents were advised they would need to furnish a written note from a Physician indicating Robert could safely return to school. Now that Robert is under psychiatric care, a note has been delivered to the school. The Psychiatrist has requested the parents to provide periodic observations of Robert's behavior from the school and to accompany Robert to the school bus each morning.

The school team advises Robert's parents that should Robert physically assault anyone at school, a transfer to an Alternative Learning Center (ALC – a school for children with serious behavioral issues) will follow. The parents, in turn, explain this potential consequence to Robert.

This is a good place to review what we've learned about underlying conditions.

What Underlying Disorders Are Common Vulnerabilities of Victims of Bullying?

In the examples above, I chose situational depression for Trey and Bipolar Disorder for Robert as underlying causes of misbehavior.

Trey's depression was caused by bullying and improved dramatically when this stress was removed. There are many other disorders that create vulnerabilities for potential victims of bullying.

Common Underlying Conditions Creating Vulnerability for Victims

There are many medical and psychiatric disorders that create vulnerabilities for victimization from bullying. In some cases, when stresses are removed from a victim of bullying, the victim becomes immune to further bullying. However, the extent of recovery depends not only on the duration, intensity and possible physical harm visited on a victim, but also on the nature of any underlying disorder. The underlying vulnerabilities of a victim of bullying may follow damage to the brain, like the effects of alcohol and other illicit drugs, exposure to toxins during pregnancy or afterward or physical trauma. In other instances, the inheritance of a disorder from a previous generation in the family may have created a victim's vulnerability. Here are some such conditions:

- Intellectual limitations/mental retardation
- Autistic spectrum disorders/social-adaptive deficits
- Genetic conditions associated with odd body appearance
- Short stature, obesity
- Stuttering/stammering
- Hearing/vision impairments
- Race/ethnicity
- Anxiety/depressive disorders

Robert's Bipolar Disorder emerged as he entered adolescence. This condition usually represents an inherited process over which an individual has only limited control. Robert will require psychotherapy to acquire coping strategies and medication to normalize brain function.

Many conditions are inherited from previous generations, including Major Depressive Disorder, Anxiety Disorder and others. No matter the origin of these disturbances, they provide a piano on which bullying and its effects are played.

Other underlying mental disorders might have been chosen as examples:

- Common mental disorders associated with bullying include-

    o Mood disorders (like Bipolar Disorder)

    o Personality Disorders (like Borderline Personality Disorder)

    o Bullying as a role model (e.g. – bullying by a parent)

    o Peer pressure (e.g. – members of a clique)

Psychologists and Psychiatrists are able to assess these cases, predict likely outcomes and treat them.

Once conditions underlying bullying have been recognized and managed and residual bad choice-making has been isolated, bullying and victimization can be redirected. In the last two chapters of this book, simple, yet powerful motivational strategies are presented in detail.

Let's Review What We've Learned in Chapter Three

Distinguish underlying disorders that block free choice-making from willful misbehavior: *see table on page 46.*

Check effects on the Performance category of the Consequence Areas to choose a professional consultant in this order:

physical > Physician, then

social > Psychologist, then

education > Educator.

Once underlying conditions are managed or eliminated and you're sure your child can take responsibility for decision-making, move on to developing a strategy.

Chapter Four

Strategies for Managing Bullies and Victims

In Chapter One, we learn that bullying may not announce itself as such to a parent. Rather, a parent must examine the effects of suspect behavior on a child's Areas of Consequence to first define a broader category of misbehavior.

At this early stage of recognition, the question a parent might pose is, "Do I need to intervene in any way?" Declines in Performance category of the Consequence Areas (consisting of *physical, social or educational* components), complaints by Others (either you or anyone else), or threats to Authority define misbehavior, though we don't know yet if we need somehow to control it or whether we can ignore it.

In Chapter Two, we show you how to answer that question by assigning objective and subjective scores to the consequences of suspect behavior, thus determining its severity. In the case of bullying, we learn to recognize and ignore teasing and how to expose and STOP life-threatening bullying with whatever means are required.

Chapter Three prompts us to recognize underlying mental and physical disorders that preclude holding children fully responsible for their acts. We learn many such conditions, like mercury poisoning, thyroid abnormalities, Bipolar Disorder and Depression, can be diagnosed and successfully treated by professional helpers, restoring children's abilities to choose appropriate behavior. We also see some conditions, like inherited short stature, intellectual deficiencies and Autistic Spectrum Disorders, though recognizable, cannot be fully reversed, but must be accommodated in developing effective strategies.

Now that we've limited bullies and victims to children who are unlikely to suffer serious harm or even death in the near future and who are capable of making better behavioral choices, let's examine various strategies for restoring them to good mental health.

The Case of James, a Teenager With Asperger Disorder

James, 15 years of age, is brought by his parents to a mental health clinic after a brief admission to a Crisis Unit (CU). His parents called **911** when James refused to leave his bedroom after 36 hours, during which time he ate only candy bars, played constantly on his computer, neglected personal hygiene and refused to go to school.

During his stay at the CU, James divulged he's being bullied at school by students in his Exceptional Student Education (ESE) classes. He related he had been planning to hang himself, though he had not yet attempted to do so. He was cooperative while in the CU, engaged with a therapist during his stay and denied having suicidal plans by the time of his discharge. He was discharged home with a scheduled appointment at the mental health clinic. No medications were prescribed.

James' history, reviewed by the psychiatrist at the clinic, is as follows:

The parents relate that James is their only child and that his Mom's pregnancy, labor and delivery were normal as were the first 3 years of his life. However, the parents do recall that by 3½ years of age, they became concerned about James' delayed speech and disinterest in playing with others.

Mom recalls James was enrolled in Pre-K at 4 years of age where his teacher reported he spent much of his time hiding under a desk, rocking. He was expelled from the school after biting a child when she approached and tried to play with him. As time went by, the parents became more concerned with James' continued avoidance of other children, the rarity of his speech, his limited vocabulary and his preoccupation with buttons.

At 5 years of age, James was enrolled in Kindergarten at the local school where his odd behaviors prompted formal testing by the School Psychologist. He was found to have normal intelligence, but his social-adaptive skills were deficient. He seemed unable to either express or comprehend emotion. His inability to respond to others' body language often resulted in rejection by peers and unintended challenges to authority. The psychologist suspected James suffered from Asperger Disorder, a mild form of autism.

James was placed in an ESE class, though he attended mainstream math and science classes. A number of school counselors worked with him through elementary and middle school, focusing on the acquisition of social skills. The parents say he made slow, but steady progress – appearing odd to classmates, but achieving average grades in most subjects and generating few complaints from his school.

Upon entry into high school, James became addicted to his computer. He was often awake until early morning hours playing games or surfing the net. Any attempt to limit his computer time resulted in rages, sometimes associated with his punching holes in walls or banging his head. James began to complain of being bullied at school. He was unwilling or unable to identify his tormentors. The parents say they complained to the school, but were told no one had actually seen any bullying.

Over the last several months, James often refused to attend school. His grades plummeted. Personal hygiene was often ignored and James lost weight. Most recently, his activities have been limited to play on the computer or video games and his rages have intensified. For the 36 hours prior to his admission to the CU, James did not emerge from his bedroom, prompting his parents to call 911. When the police arrived and advised James he would be transported to a CU for evaluation, he began throwing items at the officers. He was handcuffed and transported against his will to the Unit.

The psychiatrist praises James' parents for arranging James admission to the CU – a forceful and appropriate response to James' life-threatening behavior.

Applying the Principles We've Learned to James' Misbehavior & Victimization

A review of the effects of James' recent behavior on the Consequence Areas of Performance (*physical, social and educational*), complaints by Others, including parents and teachers, and challenges to Authority, along with the parents' reaction of FEAR, easily generates a combined objective and subjective score of 7 – 9 degrees of intensity. Though at the time of their **911** call, the parents had not heard James utter suicidal thoughts; his misbehavior within the life-endangering zone of intensity defines a risk of severe harm, either to himself or others. This level of danger requires the parents to STOP the process immediately, before any other steps can be taken. The parents might hope for James' cooperation in their efforts to manage his misbehavior, but his opposition cannot justify deferring whatever action is needed to ensure his safety and the safety of those around him.

Once safety is ensured, lowering James' point range on the Bullying Thermometer from a life-threatening to a moderate level, attention can be directed to identifying and treating or eliminating underlying causes for his behavior. Underlying physical or mental disorders, by their persistence or elimination, will determine the degree to which James will be able to take responsibility for his acts and make better behavioral choices. The parents must become aware of any such limitations to James's decision-making before they can develop realistic and effective behavioral management strategies.

Identifying James' Underlying Physical & Mental Health Disorders

With his appearance at the Psychiatrist's office following his release from the CU, James is no longer locked in his room. His parents are able to feed him adequately and supervise his personal hygiene. Still, no one doubts that without further intervention, James will likely revert to his previous patterns of behavior. After all, James has already been identified as having Asperger Disorder and his social skills and strange behavior remain barriers to his progress and confer an ongoing vulnerability for bullying.

- Asperger Disorder

The degree of habilitation of a child with an Autistic Spectrum Disorder (ASD) like Asperger Disorder is determined by the child's intellectual ability (level of comprehension) and the child's degree of motivation (willingness to acquire social skills).

The Psychiatrist confirms James' Asperger Disorder and recommends weekly counseling sessions targeting social-adaptive skills.

- Major Depressive Disorder/Anxiety Disorder

The Psychiatrist determines that James is becoming aware of the impact Asperger Disorder is having on his life. He has gradually developed feelings of depression and anger, worsened by rejection and bullying by classmates. This in turn has created intense anxiety in any social setting and has led to his frequent refusal to attend school.

Though psychotherapy is indicated to develop better insight and coping skills, the Psychiatrist feels antidepressant medication is also indicated to lessen anxiety and depression.

Constructing a Management Plan for James

James' parents recognize their son's misbehavior by its consequences (though bullying was not initially identified as a component). They count the objective effects of his behavior on the Consequence Areas and combine those with a subjective estimate of their emotional response to his behavior to quickly determine its level of intensity. Combined scores between 7 and 9 degrees justify immediate and powerful intervention to STOP a potentially life-endangering situation. The parents achieve this by calling **911**.

After removing James' from immediate danger, his parents seek professional help to identify underlying disorders. A psychiatrist discovers that James' suffers from Asperger Disorder, a mild form of Autism, but also diagnoses Anxiety and Depressive Disorders. Psychotherapy is advised to target James' computer addiction and to help him build better social skills. Therapy will also target James' anger issues. Last, medication is prescribed for short-term management of these mood disturbances.

This is the management plan proposed for James. Its goal is to quickly eliminate James' suicidal thinking and, over time, to increase his self-esteem and thus diminish his vulnerability to bullying.

Unfortunately, James refuses to engage in therapy or counseling and also refuses to take medication!

What can the parents do now?

In the next chapter, we'll show you how to get children to do what you want them to do when they're able to make conscious choices. But before we go there, let's look at another story.

The Case of Wanda, a Ten Year Old Bully

Wanda is the oldest of three children living with Mom and Stepdad. Her "real" Dad lives in another state and he calls her only rarely. Her eight year old sister and six year old brother are products of her Mom's marriage to Stepdad. Wanda has exhibited frequent anger flare-ups since she began Kindergarten – about the time her parents separated.

Stepdad has been having more and more trouble disciplining Wanda over the past two years. During temper outbursts, Wanda often yells, "You're not my Dad!" Both parents have been contending with disrespect and oppositional behavior. More recently, Wanda has been stealing money from Mom's purse, taking the belongings of her brother and sister and fabricating stories about their misbehavior. When confronted with complaints from her siblings, Wanda resorts to physical assaults. Though often caught in the act, Wanda denies any misdeeds, accusing other family members of bullying her.

Wanda's teachers have sent several notes home over the past two months. The notes detail episodes of name-calling by Wanda and some of her classmates, directed at LaQisha, a newly arrived girl. Last week, the parents were called to Wanda's school for a meeting with the principal. It seems Wanda is a member of a small group of girls who have been bullying LaQisha for the past several weeks. Wanda and members of her clique have been heard calling racial slurs at LaQisha. The parents are advised that Wanda and other members of her group are suspended from school. Consideration is being given to transferring Wanda to an Alternative Learning Center (ALC).

Applying the Principles We've Learned to Wanda's Misbehavior

Wanda's parents review of the effects of her behavior on the Consequence Areas of Performance (*physical, social and educational*), complaints by Others, including parents and teachers,

58

and challenges to teachers' Authority. Counting the objective effects of her behavior and combining these with subjective emotional response of Anxiety, the parents are able to discern a bullying score of 5 – 6 degrees of intensity. This moderate level of misbehavior requires intervention, but does allow time to develop a strategy.

There are as yet no *physical* consequences to Wanda's Performance, but the *social* and *educational* components of Wanda's Performance are affected. In choosing a professional helper to identify and manage underlying disorders, the parents recall *physical* consequences are investigated by a Physician, then *social* consequences by a Psychologist, then *educational* consequences by an Educator. In Wanda's case, there being no physical consequences, consultants are chosen in this order:

social > Psychologist, then

educational > Educator

Identifying Wanda's Underlying Disorders

At the parents' request, the School Psychologist agrees to evaluate Wanda. The psychologist determines Wanda is a bright child suffering from an Adjustment Disorder and an associated Depressive Disorder, both likely triggered by her parents' separation and divorce five years earlier. Wanda is an angry, moderately depressed child who has expressed doubt she is an accepted member of her family. She directs her anger at anyone attempting to impose limits, including parents or teachers and at any vulnerable peer. Her refusal to abide by reasonable rules at home or in school qualifies her for an additional diagnosis of Oppositional-Defiant Disorder (ODD).

Wanda's Mental Health Disorders

- Adjustment Disorder

Adjustment Disorders are triggered by stressful events in a person's life. They manifest with a variety of symptoms, including anger, depression, anxiety, loss of stamina and many others. Since, by definition, there are no underlying disturbances of brain chemistry, the outlook for full recovery is good, but depends upon the individual's motivation and commitment to engage in therapy. Therapy and counseling are usually sufficient to restore mental health, but medication may also be required in the short-term.

- Depressive Disorder

Stressful events in a person's life can cause this disorder, but it can also be caused by more serious processes, including inherited abnormalities of the brain, pregnancy-related hormone imbalances, psychotic disorders and others. Therapy and counseling may be sufficient to restore mental health, but medication for anxiety or depression is often required as well.

- Oppositional-Defiant Disorder (ODD)

A useful translation of the psychiatric diagnosis of ODD might be, "I'll do things MY way, not yours!" It's an example of a child's consistent decision to disobey.

Though Wanda's school can offer counseling services, the Psychologist advises the parents to seek more intense psychotherapy elsewhere for Wanda's mental health disorders. Also, the school team has recommended Wanda's immediate transfer to an Alternative Learning Center (ALC) for behaviorally challenged children.

Constructing a Management Plan for Wanda

Wanda's parents agree with the Psychologist that more intense work is required for Wanda than can be delivered by the school. However, they disagree with the school team's recommendation to transfer Wanda to an ALC program. They fear that Wanda, who is bright, will fall behind academically in a school for children with behavior problems. Worse, they fear Wanda's likely classmates in the ALC program will be inappropriate role models, especially for their angry, depressed and oppositional daughter. Since the school seems unwilling to consider alternative options, the parents decide they will need a School Advocate (a trained representative who specializes in working with schools to resolve service issues between parents and schools) to present their concerns to the school.

Hiring a private School Advocate can be expensive. The parents decide to get the professional help they need from the local Mental Health Clinic, where Psychiatrists, Social Workers (including School Advocates) and therapists are available and where the cost of service can be adjusted based on the family's financial ability.

At the clinic, a Child Psychiatrist evaluates Wanda and concurs with the School Psychologist's diagnoses of Adjustment Disorder, Depressive Disorder and Oppositional-Defiant Disorder. A Social Worker, acting as Wanda's School Advocate, visits the school with Wanda's parents and, with agreement between the parents and the school team, constructs a plan to allow Wanda to enroll in Virtual School (computer curriculum at home) – at first full time, then part time with the goal of returning Wanda to her public school program when the professionals declare safety issues have been resolved.

This is the management plan proposed for Wanda. It includes Virtual School, weekly psychotherapy, family therapy and, at the Psychiatrist's recommendation, the daily swallowing of an antidepressant pill by Wanda.

When presented with these plans, Wanda quickly agrees to Virtual School. However, she's never swallowed a pill and refuses to do so. She also refuses to attend weekly individual and family psychotherapy sessions! Her bullying of siblings continues in spite of stern warnings by her parents.

So what should the parents do now?

Options to Consider in Carrying Out Management Plans

In the examples we've just examined, both James and Wanda present easily recognized misbehaviors. The net we've thrown over these disturbances captures not only bullying, but also associated underlying physical or mental health conditions, some of which shield bullying from resolution and severely harm the children or others if they not recognized and controlled.

In James' case, a severe life-threatening level of misbehavior requires immediate steps to STOP its progression without regard to causes or strategies. Once its intensity is reduced, causes are sought, identified and treated. Professional helpers diagnose Asperger Disorder, a mild form of Autism, and Depressive and Anxiety

Disorders. The mood disturbances of depression and anxiety may result from either poor social skills associated with autism or victimization from bullying.

James' parents are advised to schedule psychotherapy and counseling for him and to begin administering medication. This strategy places a degree of responsibility on James to choose to carry through with these steps. His refusal to do so is a form of passive disobedience; that is, he's choosing not to do something he should be doing.

In Wanda's case, a moderate level of misbehavior is identified that can't be ignored, but which allows time for a strategy to be constructed. With professional help, Wanda's parents begin making plans for Virtual School, psychotherapy and medication. They demand she stop bullying her younger sister and brother. Wanda's refusal to swallow pills or attend psychotherapy and family therapy sessions are examples of passive disobedience; that is, she's choosing not to do things she's supposed to do. Wanda's persistent bullying of her siblings and defiance of her parents are examples of conscious though inappropriate choice-making.

Neither James nor Wanda is likely to make much progress without carrying out their assigned strategies. Their parents realize their children cannot be allowed to choose defiance, but how can they manage this misbehavior?

Disciplinary Models to Get Children to Obey

Here are some approaches the parents might consider:

- Deterrence: This is the easiest and simplest disciplinary choice. It might be phrased, "Stop [misbehaving] or [else]!" The "else" would be a punishment, like taking away computer time, going to bed early or not being allowed to play out of the house (e.g. - being grounded).

  o Pros: Not much thought required to fill in the parentheses. Most choices apply to any age child.

  o Cons: Makes an angry child more angry. Makes a depressed child more depressed.

- Deflection: This choice takes a bit more thought. Typical phrasing might be, "If you obey we'll [reward] you; if you continue to disobey you will be [punished]." Powerful rewards and punishments are presented and explained in the next chapter. In order to be effective, they must be chosen specifically for the child, hence the need to apply more thought.

  o Pros: Less anger is produced. Rewards, when earned, can reduce depression and build self-esteem.

  Most effective in the shortest time when children are actively defiant.

  o Cons: Takes more thought to construct.

- Diversion: A typical phrase is, "If you obey, you may have [reward 1] or [reward 2]." Because a child who consciously misbehaves anticipates an inappropriate reward as a consequence of the misbehavior, rewards 1 and 2 must be powerful enough to overwhelm the child's anticipated misbehavior-based reward.

  o Pros: Reduces anger and depression. Motivates a child to negotiate for more rewards and better behavior.

  o Cons: Takes more time to work. Requires deep knowledge of a child's preferences.

- Drawing: This disciplinary choice is designed for children who are misbehaving passively by choosing not to do something they're supposed to do. The phrasing is as follows: "When you [obey] you get [reward 1] and when you continue to obey [reward 2, etc.]."

  When children are experiencing an inappropriate reward by not doing something they're supposed to do, rewards 1 and 2 must be extremely powerful to create motivation to choose to behave. This is harder to achieve than redirecting the misguided motivation of active misbehavior.

  o Pros: Produces no anger or depression. Motivates a child to negotiate with parents to earn more rewards for continued good behavior.

  o Cons: Takes the longest time to work. Requires deep knowledge of a child's preferences.

How to Choose Between Deterrence, Deflection, Diversion or Drawing

Deterrence is a disciplinary choice that can result in unanticipated consequences. It's most often used by authorities who are able to pass off the results of punishment (anger and depression) to a child's nurturing caretakers. It's not an ideal model for anyone with a love relationship with a child because of its predictable creation of anger and depression. Because anger and depression often lead to retaliatory behaviors, the choice of deterrence as a disciplinary model often escalates a child's defiance and requires parents to respond with ever more intense consequences.

Deflection, using punishment to redirect misbehavior while offering a reward for better choice-making, allows a child to accept responsibility for behavioral choices. Some anger and depression are risks posed by this disciplinary choice, but in many cases of misbehavior in the upper midrange of intensity, time is of the essence and waiting for "rewards only" to bear fruit may not be practicable. Thus for active misbehavior, deflection is usually the best approach.

Less intense levels of misbehavior, in the lower midrange of intensity and bordering on the trivial, may allow for Diversion as a disciplinary choice. Its benefit lies in its ability to reduce anger and depression and its tendency to enhance self-esteem.

In the case of passive misbehavior, where a child is putting no energy into good behavior, often exerting no energy whatever, Drawing is usually the best approach. Punishment rarely creates motivation and usually provokes anger or depression, either of which may convert passive misbehavior into active defiance. Rewards, though time consuming and demanding of thought, avoid creating barriers to better choice-making, build self-esteem and entice a child to put energy into compliance.

Now let's see how Drawing can be used to entice James, with his passive non-compliance, to proceed with his parents' management strategy and how Deflection and Drawing can be used to redirect Wanda's misbehaviors.

We'll need to energize these disciplinary choices with powerful forces to achieve these goals. Ideally, we'd like to find rewards and punishments with the following characteristics:

- Can't be "taken" by a child unless "given" by a parent

- More powerful than the anticipated and inappropriate rewards of either passive or active misbehavior

- Cost little or nothing

- Available in many grades of intensity

- Considered "rewarding" whenever given and a "punitive" when denied

- Reliable contributors to self-esteem

Before moving on to Chapter Five, where we learn to construct and utilize rewards and punishments that incorporate all of the qualities listed above, let's review the steps we've just completed.

Let's Review What We've Learned in Chapter Four

In the first three chapters of this book, we:

- identified bullying, victimization and any associated misbehavior.

- judged the severity of the problem and STOPPED life-endangering levels of misbehavior while ignoring teasing.

- chose appropriate professional consultants to diagnose and treat any hidden physical or mental health disorders by examining the effects of the behavior on the *physical, social* or *educational* components of the child's Performance.

In Chapter Four, with the help of the professionals we selected, we've constructed a management plan, much of which will rely on the affected child's conscious cooperation. The scenarios presented in this chapter illustrate very typical forms of defiance on the part of both children. To gain their cooperation, we'll need to impose one or another of the following modes of discipline:

- Deterrence - "Obey or [else]."

- Deflection -"Obey and [reward], disobey and [punishment]."
- Diversion – "Obey and you may [reward 1] or [reward 2]."
- Drawing - "Obey and you may [reward 1], continue to obey and [reward 2, 3, 4…etc.]."

Chapter Five
Getting Kids to Stop Bullying
(& Misbehaving in General)

Nurturance is an umbrella term used to describe everything parents do for their children to help them grow and prosper.

The disciplinary models we examined in the last chapter, Deterrence, Deflection, Diversion and Drawing, are command engines that require fuel to work. That fuel consists of rewards and punishments which are most powerful when they're refined from Nurturance.

Nurturance consists of two parts, only one of which is suitable for disciplining kids.

Love – The Impregnable Component of Nurturance

Love is comprised of the acts parents engage in to provide food, shelter and clothing to a child consistently and under all circumstances. It's a heritage passed from one generation to the next, even when a child is acting like a monster; that is, love is independent of a child's behavior.

Love cannot always be given directly from parent to child. If a child is, indeed, acting monstrously, love may be delivered indirectly, at a parent's discretion, by proxy (e.g. - a police officer, a hospital or an agency). Denying love, even as a consequence of monstrous misbehavior, is a form of abuse.

Affection – The Contingent Component of Nurturance

Affection consists of the acts parents and others give a child as a means of communicating pleasure with the relationship. Giving affection implies delight in and approval of a child's behavior.

Affection directed at a child who is misbehaving is a form of dishonesty. It's a misguided message that might read, "I enjoy and approve of your misbehavior and I'm rewarding it!" Giving affection to a child who is misbehaving with the expectation the misbehavior will cease is an example of giving a reward before it's earned. This is the definition of a bribe.

Affection Within a Love Relationship

Within a love relationship, affection is imbued with much greater power than it carries within any other relationship. We might call affection given within a loving relationship Superaffection. For example, I might offer to buy a hamburger for your child on a visit to my office, but if you, as a parent, made the same offer, your Superaffection would trump my affectionate offer.

Superaffection, refined from Nurturance, is the high octane fuel best used to energize our disciplinary models.

Some Parents Are Scared to Make Affection Contingent on Good Behavior

Before we power up some of our disciplinary models to solve James' and Wanda's misbehaviors, as we left them in the last chapter, let's answer two frequently asked questions posed by parents when they first consider the use of affection to manage misbehavior:

- Will my child still love me if I withhold affection?

Yes - so long as a parent is there when it counts, consistently providing the essentials of healthy life, including an honest prediction of the consequences of the child's behavior.

- Could my child be too frail to accept such consequences?

No - When you checked for underlying mental or physical disorders and either eliminated or managed them, you ensured your child's capability to accept consequences.

Now let's see how Superaffection can fuel discipline. We'll choose the Deflection mode to overcome James' oppositional behaviors.

Recall that James has been removed from a bullying environment – his immediate safety is ensured. He's been diagnosed with Asperger Disorder, a mild form of Autism, Major Depressive Disorder and an Anxiety Disorder. The strategy developed by his parents, with the help of a Child Psychiatrist, includes therapy and counseling to develop better social skills for independent life as well as strategies James can use to reduce anxiety and depression. The Psychiatrist has also advised antidepressant medication.

James has refused to see a therapist and has refused to take medication.

Without carrying out the proposed strategy, James' parents realize he is likely to revert to his previous life-endangering level of misbehavior. James will be allowed to choose the means by which the strategy will be carried out, but not whether it will be completed. Since depression and anxiety pose ongoing risks for James and require close supervision, these issues require a timely solution.

Superaffection Used as Punishments & Rewards to Fuel Discipline

Since James remains at risk for suicidal thinking or acts, rewards and punishments must be powerful. We've learned that Superaffection includes all the acts parents perform for a child within a love relationship that communicate satisfaction with the child's behavior. Here's a list of some of those acts:

- Living at home rather than within a "safe" residential facility
- Eating with the family
- Shopping with parents
- James wearing clothes of his choice rather than hospital garb
- Using the family computer for games

None of these affectionate acts or series of acts is love, though they are usually perceived by a child as the most pleasant parts of nurturance. Each of them can be made contingent on appropriate behavioral decisions by a child. In James' case, should he fail to succeed with his strategy, he'd likely require hospitalization in a psychiatric facility. Posing withdrawal of some of these affectionate acts as a consequence of misbehavior is an honest portrayal of reality.

Using the Deflection Mode of Discipline to Manage James' Misbehavior

James' parents target two oppositional behaviors and construct two "engines" in the Deflection mode: Refusal to work with a therapist and refusal to take medication. Here's how the parents present the options to James.

"If you [*work with the therapist*] you may [*remain home with us*]; if you [*refuse to work with the therapist*] you will [*be admitted to an inpatient facility where a therapist will see you every day and the doctors will give you your medication*]."

In this example, James is given a choice – either to continue to receive Superaffection or to forego it. As you've learned, Deflection works more rapidly than Diversion or Drawing, but there is risk of increasing anger and depression.

Using the Drawing Mode of Discipline to Manage James' Misbehavior

For James' passive misbehavior, in which he's refusing to do something he's supposed to do, Drawing might have been considered as an alternative to Deflection. It would likely require more time to achieve results, but would pose no risk of intensifying either anger or depression. Here's what discipline in the Drawing mode would look like for James:

"When you [*take your medication for a week*] you'll get [*a monitor for the computer you've wanted*] and when you [*see the therapist for 2 weeks*] you'll get [*the rest of the computer you've wanted*]. [*As long as you continue to take your medications and see the therapist*], [*you can continue to use the computer*]."

Let's look at Wanda's more complex misbehaviors. Remember Wanda carries diagnoses of Adjustment Disorder (related to the trauma of a Stepdad taking the place of her biological Dad), Depressive Disorder and Oppositional-Defiant Disorder (ODD). She's continued to bully her younger siblings in spite of her parents'.

Misbehaviors Wanda's parents will be targeting will be her refusal to learn to swallow pills, her refusal to engage in therapy sessions and her continued bullying of her siblings. Since these

70

are examples of Wanda not doing things she's supposed to do, we'll begin with an example of discipline in the Drawing mode.

Using the Drawing Mode of Discipline to Get Wanda to Swallow Pills

To set up conditions for successful pill swallowing for a child who's never mastered this skill, the parents buy Tic Tacs (small pill-like candies), M&M's (medium-sized pill-like candies) and Good & Plenties (capsule-shaped candies). They explain that when Wanda can swallow each candy without chewing and without spitting it out, she will be able to swallow pills just like the candies. To motivate Wanda, they take her to a toy store where she's allowed to pick out a game she'd like to earn by swallowing the candies as described. The game will remain in the store till Wanda is successful, though a photograph of the game is pasted on a wall by her bed.

Here's how Wanda's refusal to swallow pills is targeted using wording in the Drawing mode and energized with Superaffection:

"When you [*swallow each candy without chewing or spitting it out*] you may [*return to the toy store and get your game*] and [*when you swallow your medicine the same way*] you'll get [*a bigger game at the toy store.*]. [*As long as you continue to take your medications*], [*you can continue to use the games*]."

The Drawing mode escapes the risk of worsening anger or depression, both of which are issues for Wanda. Time is not a critical factor for pill swallowing since Wanda can take chewable or liquid medications, though both are more expensive than pills.

An Example of Diversion to Get Wanda to Engage in Therapy Sessions

To motivate Wanda to see the therapist, her parents decide to utilize the power of sibling rivalry to power discipline within the Diversion mode. They need to be careful not to play into Wanda's stated perception of not belonging in the family. They can achieve this goal by demonstrating to Wanda her rewards will be given at a higher level than her siblings, both because she's the senior most child in the family and because she's asked to achieve a more difficult task.

Family therapy involves both parents and all three children each week. Individual therapy for Wanda is for her alone. She will need to see that choosing to engage in individual therapy pays off big time and that the payoff is bigger for her than it is for her siblings.

The advantage of the Diversion mode of discipline is its freedom from reactive depression or anger. But it requires extremely powerful rewards to be effective.

The parents set up the conditions for Diversion by taking their three children to a toy store. Each child is allowed to choose a toy they will earn after attending family therapy for two sessions. The toys are left in the store till they are earned. Wanda is allowed to choose a video player she's wanted. She may return to the store to claim the player after she's met with her therapist twice. The parents explain she will be offered the bigger, more expensive toy because seeing her therapist is harder than coming to the family meetings. Before we continue, it's worth mentioning this example uses "things" (toys and games) as affectionate responses to Wanda's successes. Other, less costly forms of affection are equally effective and include exclusive time with one or both parents, loosening limits like bedtime, longer periods of TV watching and the like.

Here's what Diversion looks like, targeting Wanda's refusal to engage in individual and family therapy:

"[*Anyone who attends family therapy twice will get the toys waiting for them at the store*]. [*When Wanda attends individual therapy twice, she may return to the store to claim her DVD* player]. [*If she continues in therapy, she may return to the store every 2 weeks to get another game for the player*]."

Wanda's bullying of her siblings is an active form of misbehavior in which she's doing something she's not supposed to do. It represents her expenditure of misdirected energy. Her parents have already inadvertently attempted to stop the bullying in the Deterrence mode of discipline; that is, "Stop [*it*] or [*else*]!" The parents have discovered what you, the reader, have already learned: Allowing a child's misguided energy to splatter against a punishment usually results in that energy ricocheting back in your face as anger.

This time, Wanda's parents choose to stop her bullying of siblings using the Diversion mode of discipline.

Using Diversion to Manage Wanda's Bullying of Her Siblings

Wanda's parents have been advised by the Psychiatrist that much of Wanda's anger derives from the fact that her younger siblings are the offspring of her Stepdad and her Mom, whereas her Dad lives elsewhere. Wanda's perception is that her siblings are loved more by her Stepdad than she. In constructing discipline in the Diversion mode, the parents strive to improve the relationship Wanda has with Stepdad. They know Wanda has repeatedly asked to go to Disney World. Here's the Diversion engine Mom presents to Wanda:

"Your Stepdad is planning to go to Disney World next month. He's also planning to go camping. [*If there are no complaints from your brother or sister about bullying, would you like to go with Stepdad to Disney World while I stay home with your brother and sister*] or [*would you rather go camping with all of us if there are complaints?*]

As in all cases of Diversion, anger and depression are bypassed as consequences of this mode. An added advantage to Wanda of this choice of Superaffection is the potential for an improved relationship with Stepdad.

Let's Review What We've Learned in Chapter Five

In the preceding chapters, we recognized bullying and any of its accompanying disorders and limited it to a moderate level of intensity. We took some time to develop a management plan, often with the help of professionals. Then we chose among several disciplinary models to motivate a child to comply with the plan: Deterrence, Deflection, Diversion or Drawing.

In this chapter, we've learned how to energize our chosen form of discipline to compel a child who is free to make choices to accept and implement our chosen strategy. We've seen that affection, the contingent part of love, will provide the fuel for our disciplinary engine. And we've seen that for parents, Superaffection (affection generated from a love relationship), is the highest octane fuel available.

Chapter Six

Some Final Thoughts – Putting It All Together

Why Go to the Trouble of Checking Bullying for Hidden Conditions?

As you've learned, bullying rarely travels alone. Sometimes, stressful events in a child's life create hidden mental health disorders. Other times, medical or psychiatric conditions create vulnerabilities upon which chance events play. These traveling companions of bullying or victimization, if unrecognized and untreated, make resolution of the bullying difficult or impossible. The steps you've seen applied to misbehavior in general cast a wide enough net to capture any potential companions of bullying.

Why Are Consequences So Important to Discipline?

Beside the failure to recognize and manage mental health or physical disorders accompanying bullying, another impediment to controlling this form of aggression is the misconception that holding children responsible for the consequences of their acts will somehow threaten love relationships. Forgotten is the fact that all authority figures, parents included, derive their credibility (and thereby their power) from the accuracy of their prediction of the consequences of children's behavioral choices. When likely consequences are potentially life-threatening, authorities have the obligation to substitute meaningful and instructive, though safe, consequences in their stead.

Children are always testing rules to check out their honesty. When parents accurately predict the consequences of adherence or rejection of rules, they affirm to children the value of rules as guides to behavioral choices. By contrast, when the consequences of defiance vary from those predicted by authorities, rules are justifiably ignored. Dishonest predictions of consequences encourage rule-breaking.

The Difference Between Bribes and Rewards

When parents offer rewards before they're earned, or worse, in response to misbehavior, they are engaged in bribery. Rewarding good behavior once it has occurred is not only appropriate, but necessary to validate the good behavior and to encourage its continuation.

I've heard parents ask, "Why should I reward my child for doing what is right?" The answer requires some understanding of psychotic ("crazy") behavior. One apt definition of psychotic behavior is acting without (a) reason. The reason a sane child chooses one behavior over another is the child anticipates a desirable (rewarding) outcome. Any parent who expects a child to act without an anticipated reward is asking for psychotic behavior. Or, to put it bluntly, asking a child to act without reason is asking for crazy behavior!

More About Firing Schools

When a child is being bullied, it's not unreasonable for parents to request the school to intervene. The intervention might take the form of a conference with the parents of the perpetrator(s). It could take the form of adult supervision in the immediate vicinity of the victim. It might precipitate action by the school to suspend, even transfer or expel the bully.

Sometimes, a school will not undertake any serious intervention. In cases where no physical assault has occurred, but rather verbal harassment comprises the bullying, a school's response may be ineffective or half-hearted. In such situations, it may be necessary to "fire" the school and move a child to another school. These are situations that can benefit from the services of a School Advocate.

More About School Advocates

School Advocates are individuals who are trained to work as intermediaries between schools and families. They should be considered employees of the family. Unlike school counselors, School Advocates do not contend with mixed allegiances. That is, they represent the needs and goals of the family and the child. When conflict arises between a school and a family, the School Advocate will often propose solutions outside the typical school offerings. Unlike the school staff, School Advocates offer choices to the family that take into consideration legalities, finances, psychological and educational requirements, without being bound by the school's budget or political constraints. For example, a recommendation might be made to enroll in a private school outside the public arena.

School Advocates can be found in a variety of settings. Some work out of community mental health agencies. Others may work as private consultants. Still others may be hospital-based. Various law groups advertise capabilities as educational advocates. Advocates for children with specific disabilities or medical or psychiatric disorders can be located through organizations and societies whose focus is those specific disorders.

Putting it All Together – How to Manage Bullying

Here are the simple, but powerful steps you've learned to recognize and manage bullying and any associated physical or mental disorders:

1. Check the effects of any suspect behavior on the Consequence Areas to determine if it's misbehavior:

    - Effects on the child's Performance

        o *physical*

        o *social*

        o *educational*

    - Effects on Others – yourself or anyone else

    - Effects on Authority relationships

    If any component of the Consequence Areas is affected, you've identified abnormal behavior.

2. Count the number of affected Consequence Areas to score objective points- *see Consequence Areas diagram p. 28.*

    - Performance effects – up to 3

        o *physical*   = 1

- o *social* = 1
- o *educational* = 1
- Others- up to 2
  - o You =1
  - o Anyone else =1
- Authority- up to 1

Estimate the intensity of your emotional response to score subjective points- *see thermometer on page 30.*

- *annoyance* =1
- *Anxiety, Anger, Confusion* =2
- *FEAR* =3

Add the objective and the subjective scores to determine the degree of intensity of the misbehavior.

3. Identify, manage or eliminate underlying physical or mental health disorders that take away a child's capacity to make choices: *see Table on page 46.*

    If you suspect an underlying condition, choose professionals to diagnose and treat the condition in this order:

    physical > Physician, then

    social > Psychologist, then

    education > Educator

    Construct a management plan, with professional help if necessary, to stop bullying or victimization and any associated conditions.

4. Choose a disciplinary model to motivate your child to carry out the plan:
    - Deterrence - "Obey or [else]."

- Deflection - "Obey and [reward], disobey and [punishment]."

- Diversion - "Obey and you may [reward 1] or [reward 2]."

- Drawing - "Obey and you may [reward 1], continue to obey and [reward 2, 3, 4…etc.]."

5. Energize the chosen disciplinary model with affection or, if you're a parent, with Superaffection.

Suggested Reading / Resources

Websites

1. http://www.bullyingandthelaw.org/Pages/students.cfm
2. http://www.stopbullying.gov/what-is-bullying/
3. http://www.internetsafety101.org/upload/Cyberbullying.pdf
4. http://www.nasponline.org/resources/bullying/Bullying_Primer.pdf

Books & Essays

1. Mookey the Monkey Gets Over Being Teased, H Lonczak & M Ramse
2. Bullying Prevention: Creating a Positive School Climate and Developing Social Competence, P Orpinas, PhD, MPH & A M Horne, PhD
3. Bullying Beyond the Schoolyard: Preventing and Responding to Cyberbullying, S Hinduja, J W Patchin, SAGE Publishing
4. Hey, Back Off! Tips for Stopping Teen Harassment, J/H Withers
5. Cyber-Bullying: Issues and Solutions for the School, the Classroom and the Home, S Shariff

Videos

1. http://www.stopbullying.gov/respond/be-more-than-a-bystander
2. http://www.kidpower.org/library/videos/

3. http://www.pacer.org/bullying/video/

4. http://www.greatschools.org/parenting/bullying/4217-How-to-know-if-you-child-is-being-bullied-video.gs

About the Author

Dr. Alan Davick, a Developmental-Behavioral Pediatrician, has taught parents and professional colleagues how to recognize and manage complex misbehavior in children for 40 years. Trained at the Johns Hopkins Medical Institutions and maintaining clinical practice throughout those years, Dr. Davick has focused his knowledge and experience on separating innate conditions like ADHD, Autistic Spectrum Disorders including Asperger Disorder, Bipolar Disorder, Cerebral Palsy, Developmental Delay and Psychogenic Non-Epileptic Seizures masquerading as willful misbehavior, from willful misconduct, like Oppositional-Defiant Disorder.

In ***Bullying: Rarely Travels Alone***, Dr. Davick shows you how to recognize and manage hidden physical and mental health disorders, some of which are mentioned above, which fuel bullying and victimization. He guides you through simple steps to recognize bullying and its underlying causes, judge its severity, utilize professional assistance when necessary, develop a management strategy and get your child to carry out the strategy.

Dr. Davick practices Behavioral-Developmental Pediatrics in Southwest Florida, where he lives with his wife, Barbara.

Ordering Information

Bullying: Rarely Travels Alone
Alan M. Davick, M.D.
© 2014 Alan M. Davick, M.D.
ISBN: 978-09890053-2-6

Managing Misbehavior in Kids: The MIS/Kidding Process® – A Professionals' Manual
Alan M. Davick, M.D.
© 2013 Alan M. Davick, M.D.
ISBN: 978-09890053-0-2

MISKIDDING, LLC
P.O. Box 101127
Cape Coral, FL 33910-1127

URL: www.DrDavick.com
Email: miskidding1@gmail.com

Dr. Davick's books are also available at Amazon.com and other online booksellers.

Alan M. Davick, M.D.

www.ingramcontent.com/pod-product-compliance
Lightning Source LLC
Chambersburg PA
CBHW071419040426
42445CB00012BA/1221